THIS BOOK IS A GIFT TO
the Pittsburg Library

in loving memory of
Norma Krieg
Pittsburg School Teacher

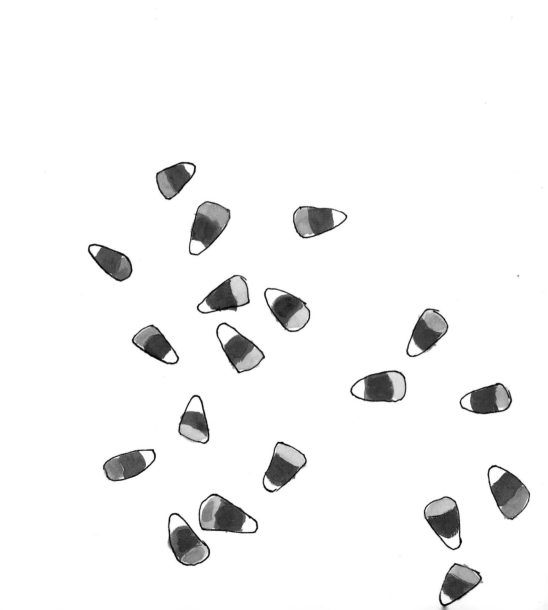

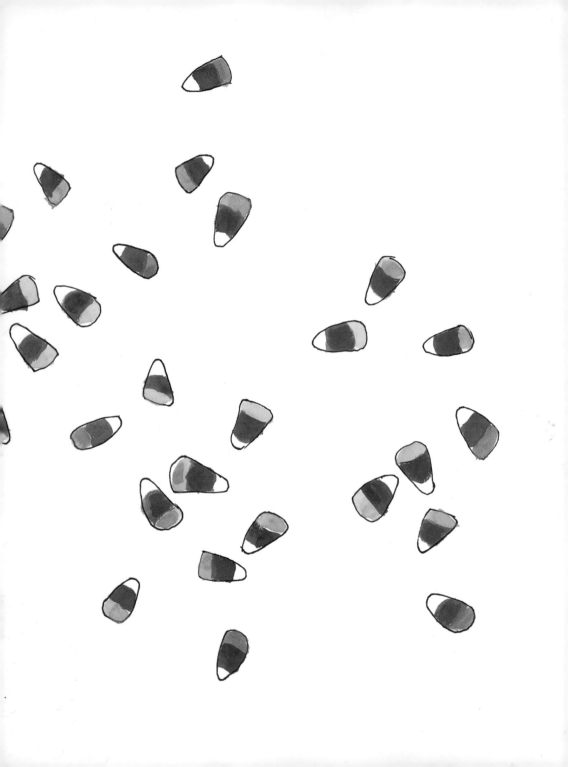

Candy Corn

POEMS BY
JAMES STEVENSON

with illustrations by the author

Greenwillow Books

New York

Watercolor paints and a black pen
were used to prepare the full-color art.

Printed in Hong Kong by South China
Printing Company (1988) Ltd.
First Edition
10 9 8 7 6 5

Library of Congress
Cataloging-in-Publication Data

Stevenson, James, (date)
Candy corn / by James Stevenson.
       p.   cm.
Summary: A collection of short
poems with titles such as
"The Morning After Halloween,"
"Dumpsters," and "What Frogs
Say To Each Other."
ISBN 0-688-15837-4
1. Children's poetry, American.
[1. American poetry.]
I. Title.   PS3569.T4557C36
1999   811'.54—dc21
98-2965   CIP   AC

For Oona and Morgan, with love

Contents

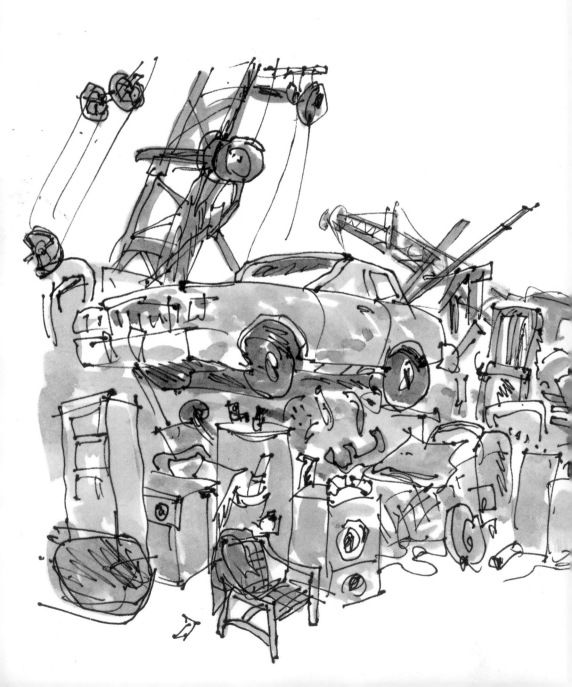

THERE'S A YELLOW CHAIR

AT THE JUNKYARD GATE.

SOMETIMES AN OLD GUY SITS THERE

JUST TO MAKE SURE

NOBODY SWIPES A CRANE.

At the edge of the woods

The dogwoods are blooming

Like white surf tumbling

From a light green sea.

First I had
this one.

Then I had this one.

Then I had
these two

and this one

and this

and this

and this, and

after that I had all of these, one after the other,

and this, too,

and then suddenly

they were all—

gone!

That's the way it is
with peanuts.

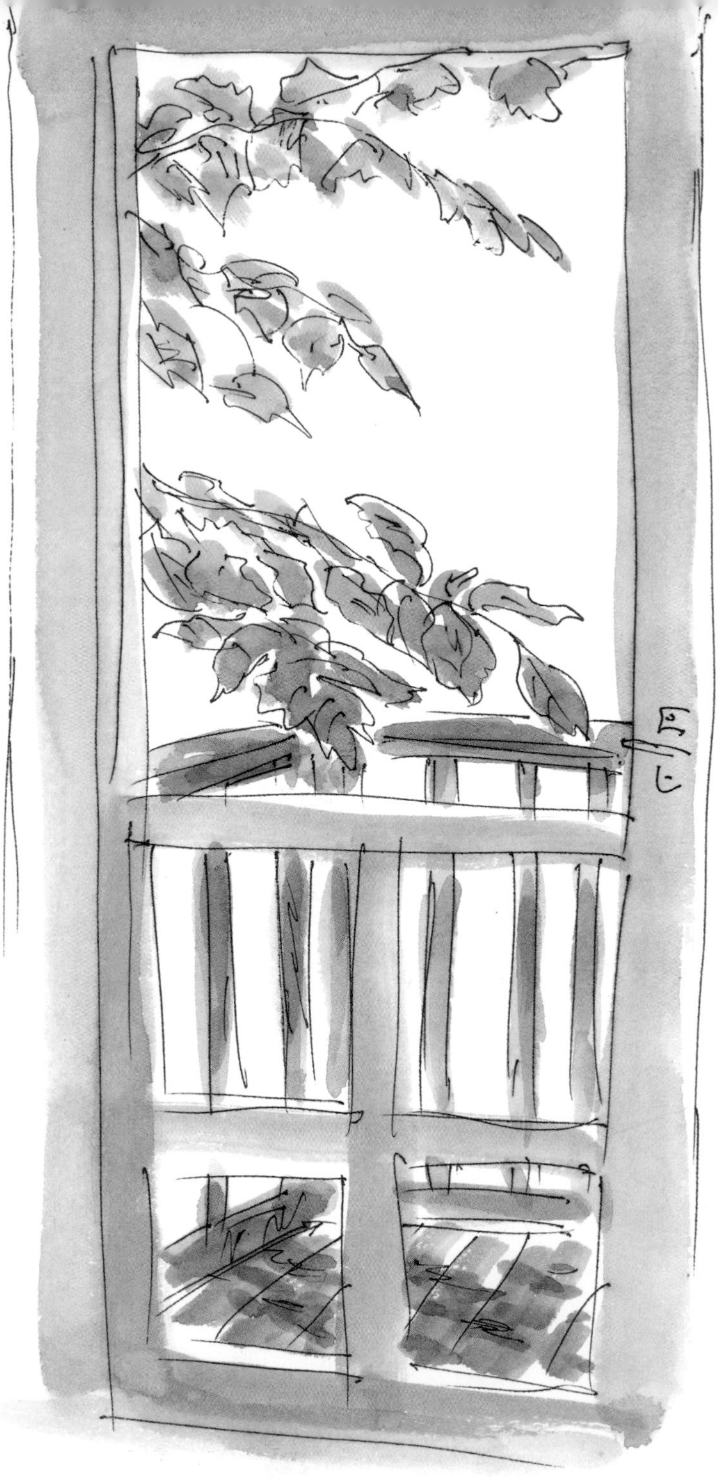

It's a friendly time of year—
Soft air, and lilacs bending
Low enough to sniff.
Even the beech tree
Has sent a branch
To pay a visit to my porch.

Twitter-twitter

Screech

Gulp

Chee-chee-chee

Aw Aw Aw

Brrrt Brrrt

Chaychit-chaychit

WEEP WEEP

C'maw C'maw

Churp Churp

Weeeeet!

Sometimes I wish I spoke Bird.

If there were just one daisy in the world,

People would line up for miles

To get a look.

But we're in luck,

And there are meadows-full right now.

You could even take some home.

BARE FEET?

NEAT!

The screen door screeches.

The screen door slams.

Coming or going,

Going or coming,

The sounds are the same.

But what a difference
It makes to me—
Your going away,
Your coming home.

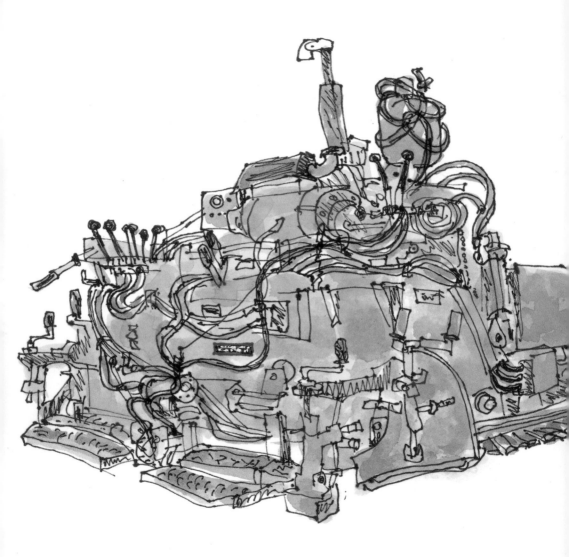

The amazing paving machine
Sits in the dirt
Not far from the highway—
Part tank, part spaghetti.
On the back is a small red sign:

DO NOT OPERATE OR TOW
THIS MACHINE WITHOUT FIRST FULLY
UNDERSTANDING THE CONTENTS OF
THE OPERATOR'S MANUAL.

But where *is* the operator?
At home, I guess, still trying
To understand
The manual.

There's a building on the drawbridge.

I'm not sure what it's for—

Maybe a swell hotel for trolls.

They probably need their rest at night—
Growling all day long.

"What's it like today—hot?"

"Only when you first get out."

Along the rusty railroad track
A building stands
That must have been important once.
Now rain goes through the open doors,
Vines climb up the walls.
Nobody ever goes there now.
But maybe the ghost of a railroad man
Waits at a window when midnight comes,
Looking at his golden pocket watch
And peering down the tracks,
Watching for a headlight coming on,
Listening for the whistle of the 12:04.

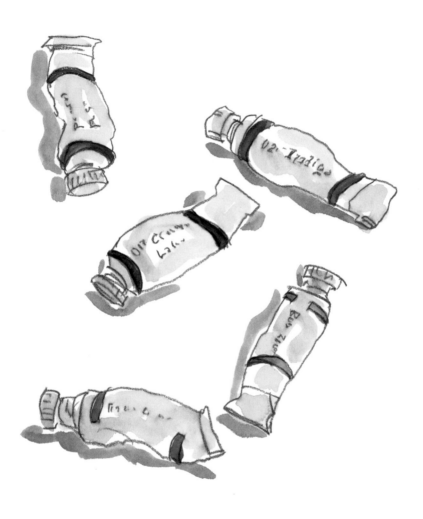

When the sky turns Indigo,

Winsor and Newton

And Permanent Rose

Will take a picnic

To Crimson Lake

And dine on slightly Burnt Sienna

And drink a French Ultramarine

Till the moon comes up

With a Lemon Yellow Hue.

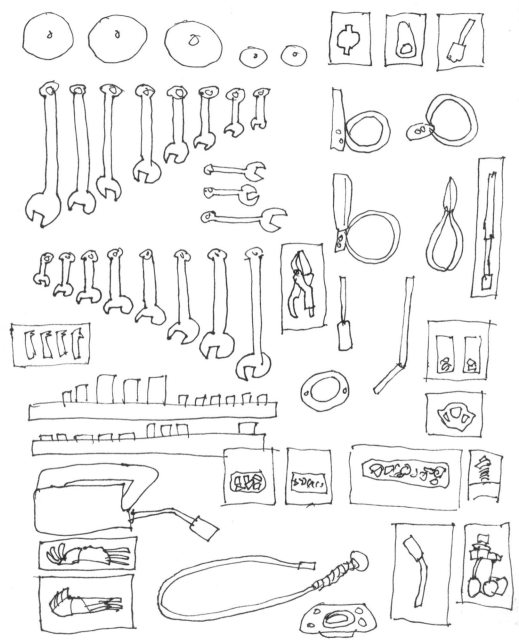

They have a lot of items at the Auto Parts store...

but I don't have a clue what they're for.

The old dry branches

Gather around the trunk

Of the big oak tree

And talk about

When they were up above,

Riding the wind,

Waving banners of green.

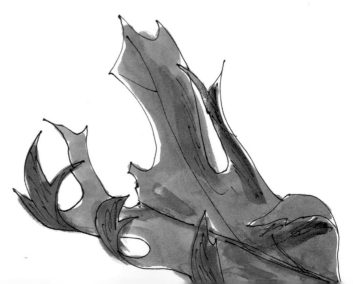

When the moment comes
When you can tell
The sky is blue, not black,
You'll see torn bits of it
Scattered through the trees,
Fallen like confetti,
As if to say
Night is not forever—

In fact, within one hour,
A grand parade is coming
With white clouds marching.

As morning comes,

You can see last night

The dragon lost

A lot of teeth.

Scattered

Along the sidewalk,

Yellow and orange they are,

Very much

Like candy corn.

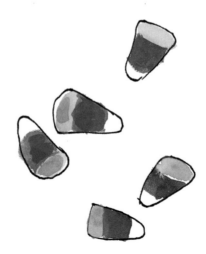

The fiery pumpkin beside the door
Has turned to mush,
Its burnt-out candle
Lying on the ground
Like some old geezer's stogie.

We're going to have burgers,

We're going to have fries,

We're going to have apple pie

With ice cream on top,

We're going to have pancakes,

Big stacks of pancakes

In puddles of syrup—

That's what we'll have

When Bob gets

Here.

I wish he'd hurry up.

On Main Street, everybody carries something.

An umbrella

A baby

A chair

A paper bag

Some cleaning

A lollipop

A child

A purse

A coat

Some shopping

A drink

A hat

A shirt

A box

A letter

A candy bar

They all carry
something.

Well, almost
everybody.

For every head

There is a hat,

A perfect hat

For every head.

Just keep looking.

A strong stone wall
Is good to see:

All those different rocks
Working together,
Getting along fine.

"What a day! I'm glad *that's* over."

"My kids just wouldn't sit still."

"Mine were yelling the whole time."

"Maybe tomorrow will be better."

"Hope so."

"Good night, 74."

"Good night, 82."

"Good night, 71."